PREFACE.

The Publishers of my Pianoforte School* have expressed to me a wish that I would explain, under the epistolary form, and in a concise, clear, and familiar manner, the peculiar mode of proceeding in the instruction of my pupils, and of leading them forwards step by step, which I have employed during my long career as a teacher of the pianoforte; and that, in so doing, I would fully detail all those minute particulars which, from their nature, could not well find a place in a pianoforte school.

By means of the present work, I have endeavoured to satisfy their request; and I have done so the more willingly, because the form

---

* The work here alluded to is Czerny's celebrated School for the Pianoforte, which is now in course of publication by Messrs. Cocks and Co. and which is, beyond all comparison, the most extensive and complete method for that instrument ever published.

of Letters approximates the nearest to verbal instruction.

The reader must suppose, therefore, that, by means of short, friendly, and cheerful letters, I have undertaken to draw the attention of a talented and well-educated girl of about twelve years old, residing at a distance in the country, progressively to every thing which might assist her in the better comprehension and application of the rules which are contained in almost every pianoforte school.

It is further assumed that each letter follows that which immediately preceded it, after a lapse of about eight or ten weeks; so that the pupil may have sufficient intermediate time to learn all the rules which are laid down, and to avail herself of them in her subsequent practice.

And thus the instructions here given proceed gradually and naturally from the earliest rudiments to the highest degree of cultivation; for the last letters contain as much explanation relative to the principles of Harmony or Thorough-bass as the limits of this little work would allow, in order to facilitate and render intelligible to the pupil any future study of the theory of music.

I hope, therefore, that a frequent and attentive perusal of this little work, and an intelligent application of the rules given therein, will prove of utility to pupils of every age, and in every stage of their progress; since I have endeavoured, in them, to avoid as far as possible the dryness so generally complained of in works of instruction, and to place every subject within the comprehension of a pupil of whatever age.

Though these Letters are written as a kind of Appendix to my own Pianoforte School, still they may be used with equal advantage along with any other *Method;* and may therefore, perhaps, be considered as a not unwelcome assistance to pupils in general.

C. CZERNY.

CONTENTS.

LETTER I.
First Rudiments of the Piano.. 1

LETTER II.
On Touch, Tone, and the Mode of Treating the Pianoforte 10

LETTER III.
On Time, Subdivision of the Notes, and Fingering 18

LETTER IV.
On Expression, and Graces or Embellishments........ 27

LETTER V.
On the Keys, on Studying a Piece, and on Playing in the presence of others........................... 35

LETTER VI.
On the Selection of Compositions most suitable for each Pianist............................. 43

LETTER VII.
Rudiments of Thorough-bass...... 51

LETTER VIII.
On the Formation of Chords...................... 62

LETTER IX.
Continuation of Thorough-bass.. 70

LETTER X.
On Extemporaneous Performance................... 72

LETTER I.

FIRST RUDIMENTS OF THE PIANO.

Miss Cecilia,

  When I, some years ago, had the pleasure of being personally acquainted with your family, I discovered in you so decided a talent for music, that I am exceedingly rejoiced to hear that you are now really about to devote yourself to the delightful art of playing the pianoforte. Your memory, at that time, easily retained any agreeable melody which you heard; you manifested a natural feeling for time and musical expression; and, added to this, your delicate fingers and hands possessed all the natural qualities so necessary for playing the pianoforte—flexibility, quickness of movement, and lightness, without being either too weak or too stiff.

  So decided a disposition and inclination for this fine art could not, in truth, remain long dormant; for no art is more noble, nor more surely indicative of general mental cultivation than music; and you know that *pianoforte playing*, though suitable to every one, is yet more particularly one of the most charming and honorable accomplishments for young ladies, and, indeed, for the female sex in general. By it we can command, not only for one's self, but for many others, a dignified and appropriate amusement; and, where great progress has been made, we also ensure a degree of distinction in the world, which is as agreeable to the amateur as to the professional artist.

As, on account of the distance of your residence, I cannot, alas! satisfy the wish of your honored parents by undertaking your instruction in person; I, with pleasure, impose it on myself as a duty, to urge you, from time to time by letters, to still greater diligence, and also to direct your attention, according to my own views, to all that may facilitate your tuition, and accelerate your *progress*; though, on the part of the very respectable master to whom your instruction is confided, all will unquestionably be done to cultivate your talent in a way equally tasteful and solid.

I beg of you, therefore, Miss Cecilia, to look upon my remarks merely as an *explanatory repetition* of what will have already been delivered to you, either verbally or in my Pianoforte School; and my end will be fully attained, if by this means your zeal is augmented, and the time and labor of learning abridged and facilitated.

The first principles, namely, a knowledge of the keys and of the notes, are the only really tedious and unpleasant points in learning music. When you have once conquered them, you will every day experience more and more amusement and delight in continuing your studies.

Consider the matter, dear Miss Cecilia, as if you were for a time compelled to wend your way among somewhat tangled and thorny bushes, in order to arrive at last at a beautiful prospect, and a spot always blooming in vernal beauty.

The best remedy against this disagreeable necessity is, to endeavour to fix these preliminary subjects on your memory as firmly and quickly as possible. Such pupils as manifest from the very outset a desire and love for the thing, and who strongly and rationally apply their memories to the matter, will acquire a perfect knowledge of the keys and notes in a few weeks; while others, frightened at the apparent tediousness of the acquisition, often lose several months in attaining the same object. Which, then, of these two ways is the better?

Before any thing else, I earnestly entreat you, Miss Cecilia, to acquire a graceful and appropriate position, when sitting at the pianoforte. The seat which you use must be just so high that the elbows, when hanging down freely, may be a very little less elevated than the upper surface of the keys; and if your feet should not reach the ground, have a dwarf stool or ottoman made, of a proper height, to place them upon. You must always seat yourself exactly facing the middle of the key-board, and at such a distance from it that the tips of the elbows may be a little nearer to the keys than the shoulders.

Equally important is a graceful position and carriage of the head and upper part of the chest; it must neither be stiff nor bent. Some of my former little pupils, whom I used to teaze with the reproach of *making a cat's back*—that is, sitting with their backs bent and oblique—have, in later days, thanked me for the strictness which I shewed in this particular.

It is not merely that an awkward position is disagreeable and ridiculous, but it also impedes, if not prevents, the development of a free and elegant style of playing.

The fore part of the arm (from the elbow to the fingers) should form a perfectly straight horizontal line, for the hand must neither rise upwards like a ball, nor be bent so as to slope downwards.

The fingers are to be so bent that the tips of them, together with that of the thumb, when extended outwards, may form one right line; and so that the keys may always be struck with the soft and fleshy tips of the fingers, and that neither the nails nor the flat surface of the fingers shall touch the keys. In striking the black keys, the fingers must be stretched out a little more; but even in this case they must always remain sufficiently bent.

The percussion on the keys is effected solely by the fingers, which, without any actual blow, must press each key firmly down; and in doing this, neither the hand nor the arm must be allowed to make any unnecessary movements. The thumb should always strike the key with its external narrow surface, and in so doing it must be but very little bent.

The white keys are to be struck on the middle of their anterior broad surfaces, and the black keys pretty close to their nearest extremities or ends.

You must take great care, Miss, that you do not strike any key sideways or obliquely; as, otherwise, a contiguous and wrong key may chance to be touched; and, in music, nothing is worse than *playing wrong notes.*

While one finger strikes, the other fingers must be kept close to the keys, but always bent, and poised quite freely in the air; for we must not touch any key before the moment in which it is to be struck.

The most important of the fingers is the

thumb; it must never be allowed to hang down below the key-board; but, on the contrary, it should always be held *over* the keys in such a way that its tip may be elevated a little higher than the upper surface of the black keys; and it must strike from this position.

To observe all these rules exactly, it is requisite that the elbows should never be too distant from the body; and that the arms, from the shoulder downwards, should hang freely, without being pressed against the body.

The necessity of all these rules you will not be able to comprehend till a future period.

The knowledge of the notes is a mere affair of memory; and for every note you must endeavour to find and strike the proper key, on the instant and without the least hesitation. In music, this constitutes what is called *reading the notes;* and when you shall have acquired this readiness, you will have overcome the most difficult thing which elementary objects in music will be likely to present to you.

At first, you will naturally learn only the notes in the treble clef; and for this purpose we may employ the following means:

First. When you look at a note, you must name it aloud, and then seek for and strike the key which belongs to it.

Secondly. When you strike at hazard any white key on the treble side of the key-board, you must name it aloud, and seek directly for the note belonging to it.

Thirdly. After having struck any white key at hazard, you must describe aloud, in words, on what line or in what space the note belonging to it must be written.

Fourthly. You must often play slowly through some of the easiest pieces for beginners, note by note, and with great attention, naming each note as you proceed.

Fifthly. I must also recommend you, Miss, to adopt the following expedient: since you are already much advanced in writing, as it becomes a young female of education to be, you must learn to write music. The little trouble that this will cost, you will find amply recompensed by great advantages. Notes are much easier to write than letters; and, if you daily devote a short quarter of an hour to this task, in a couple of weeks you will become sufficiently expert at it.

Your teacher will give you the instructions requisite for this purpose; and when you have been in this way accustomed to place the notes as they come, exactly on or between the lines, copy out daily one of the easiest elementary lessons, and then write in letters over each note its proper denomination; after which, play the piece over slowly.

When, in this way, you have learned to

know perfectly all the notes in the treble clef, and are able to play slowly, but correctly, with both hands, all those little pieces in my School, which are written for both hands in the treble clef, then take the bass notes, and proceed with them just in the same manner.

You must practise each piece, paying the strictest attention to the fingering indicated, till you are able to execute it without stopping or stumbling. Each day you should read through a couple of fresh little pieces, to accustom the eye and the fingers to the various and ever-new passages which are formed by means of the notes.

At first, after each note, we must also look at the key which is to be struck; but afterwards, when we have attained a tolerable certainty in finding the keys, it is better to fix the eye on the notes rather than on the keys.

And now, Miss, allow me in this letter to offer this last very important remark: the best knowledge of the notes avails us very little, if, *at the same time*, the fingers do not begin to develop that degree of flexibility which is requisite for striking the keys and for playing in general. I therefore most earnestly recommend you to practise daily, with untiring diligence and the greatest attention, all the five-finger exercises in both hands, which you will find at the beginning of my Pianoforte School, and which your instructor will explain to you; in order that your small and delicate, though still sufficiently powerful fingers, may speedily acquire that pliability, independence, and volubility which is absolutely necessary to playing.

Do not be alarmed at the little trouble and application that this may require; try three or four times every day, for at least a quarter of an hour each time, to play through these exercises with attention. In fact, it is as impossible to play the pianoforte well with stiff and untractable fingers, as to dance well with stiff and untractable feet. *Volubility of finger is one of the chief requisites in pianoforte-playing.*

It is very proper that your teacher gives you an hour's lesson every day. If, in addition to this, you daily dedicate another hour—or, if possible, two hours to practising by yourself—you will in a few months have for ever conquered all that is difficult or tedious in the elementary branches of playing; and you will each day see augmented the pleasure which the delightful art of music so richly bestows on its votaries.

And now, Miss CECILIA, farewell; and rejoice soon with the intelligence of your progress,

Your most devoted, &c.

LETTER II.

(TWO MONTHS LATER.)

ON TOUCH, TONE, AND THE MODE OF TREATING THE PIANOFORTE.

My dear Miss,

I have just received your welcome letter, and learn from it that you have already made a notable progress in reading the notes, and that you are able to play several of the first and easiest little pieces, somewhat slowly perhaps, but still intelligibly.

Continue daily to decypher a couple of new little pieces, and at the same time to practise still more those which you have already learned, so that these latter ones may go off quicker and quicker, and that you may each week study at least two fresh pieces. For, as you have an earnest wish to attain to a high degree of excellence in pianoforte-playing, you must look upon all that has been given to you as yet, only as a *means to that end*, and, indeed, as that means which will conduct to this end *as quickly and as agreeably as possible*.

I could not refrain from laughing a little, if I may be allowed to tell you so, at your complaining to me how much your master vexed and tormented you with finger-exercises, with rules relating to touch, to the position of the hands, to clearness, volubility, &c. &c.

"Ah!" exclaim you, in a manner quite touching, " must all this really be so ?"

Yes—such is indeed the case; and here, dear Miss, I cannot assist you; your worthy teacher is quite right in being so strict as to all these points, and I will explain the reason why. From every musical instrument we may produce either a fine tone or a detestable one, *according as we handle it*. The same excellent violin which, in the hands of a clever player, sounds so delightfully, will, when handled by a clumsy person, yield as disagreeable sounds as if a number of kittens were squalling. It is the same with the pianoforte. If it is not properly handled by the player, or if we merely thump and bang the keys, the best instrument will sound hard and unpleasant. On the other hand, if we employ too little force, or do not know how to use this power in a proper manner, the tone will be poor and dull, and the performance unintelligible, and without soul or expression.

The interior mechanism of the keys is such that the strings will only sound well when we—

First. Strike each key perpendicularly; that is, straight downwards, and exactly in the middle, and therefore not sideways nor obliquely.

Secondly. When, after the percussion, each key is so firmly pressed down as to cause the full tone of the instrument to be audible.

Thirdly. When, before the percussion, we do not raise the finger too high; as otherwise, along with the tone, there will be heard the blow on the key.

Fourthly. When the hand and arm, even when striking with considerable force, do not make any jumping, chopping, or oscillating movement. For you will find, Miss, that the fingers cannot possibly play pleasantly and tranquilly when the hands and arms are unsteady.

Fifthly and lastly. When the player observes all these rules in rapid runs, or even in skips and extensions, as strictly as in slow and quiet passages.

All the finger-exercises, and particularly the *scales*, have no other end than to accustom the fingers to the application of these rules so thoroughly, that the player shall practise all that he studies in future strictly according to the principles we have given.

" *Ah! the scales,*" you write to me; " *that* is truly a tedious story ! Are these things then really as necessary as my teacher says ?"

Yes, Miss Cecilia, these scales are the *most*

necessary point of all, not only for beginners, but even for pupils who are much advanced; and, indeed, the most expert players do and must constantly have recourse to and practise them. Permit me to demonstrate this to you, as I know that you have a good understanding, and are fond of reflecting.

You know already that the passing of the thumb *under* the other fingers, and of the three middle fingers *over* the thumb, is absolutely necessary, and that it is the only means by which we are enabled to strike a long series of keys quickly one after the other.

But this passing of the thumb and fingers, even in the most rapid passages, must be effected in a manner so natural, equal, and unlaboured, that the hearer shall not be able to distinguish the smallest interruption or inequality. This, however, is almost the greatest difficulty in pianoforte-playing; and it is possible only when neither the arm nor the hand makes the smallest movement upwards or sideways, and when the joints of all the fingers attain gradually and by long practice so great a degree of flexibility and address, that in a rapid run over the key-board one is almost tempted to think that the player has at least fifty fingers on each hand. To attain this highly necessary property, there is no other means than the most diligent, uninterrupted daily practice of the scales in all the keys, as you will find them given in a connected arrangement in my Pianoforte School, and illustrated by the requisite explanations.

But these scales have many other various uses. There are few musical compositions in which they are not introduced by the author in some shape or other. In every piece, whether written to day or one hundred years ago, they are the principal means by which every passage and every melody is formed. The diatonic scales, or the chords broken into arpeggios, you will every where find employed innumerable times.

You will now easily imagine, Miss, what an advantage it gives a player when he is perfectly acquainted, in all the keys, with these FUNDAMENTAL PASSAGES, from which so many others are derived; and what a command over the entire key-board, and what an easy insight into any musical piece he gains thereby.

Farther, no property is more necessary and important to the player than a well-developed *flexibility, lightness, and volubility* of the fingers. This cannot be acquired in any way so quickly as by the practice of the scales. For, if we were to try to attain those qualities by the merely studying of different musical compositions, we should spend whole years to accomplish our purpose. Many beautiful pieces require to be executed in a very quick degree of movement, and with great volubility of finger. But how tiresome and detestable would not these same pieces sound, if played slow, stiff, and unequal! And even those compositions which are slow on the whole, still contain many occasional runs and embellishments which require great rapidity of finger. All these *he* has *already* conquered who is able to play the scales well and with sufficient quickness.

At present, Miss Cecilia, you cannot form an idea of the beauty and effect which is produced by a pure, clear, rapid, and *strictly equal* execution of such runs; they are musical rows of pearls; and many great artists are more particularly distinguished on account of their peculiar excellence in the performance of them. You will no doubt have already remarked, that correct *fingering* is a very important part of pianoforte playing, and one which costs every pupil a good deal of labour. Now, the scales contain all the principal rules of fingering; and they are in themselves sufficient, in almost all cases, to shew the pupil the right path. What do you say to all these advantages? Is it not well worth the while to occupy yourself seriously with these same tiresome scales?

I must now tell you in *what way* you ought to proceed to do this. For, if *studied in a wrong manner*, the scales may prove as injurious as they are capable of being serviceable when properly practised. You know, Miss, that the five fingers are by no means equal to each other in natural strength. Thus, for example, the thumb is much stronger than any of the other fingers; the first finger is much stronger than the little finger, and the third finger, on the contrary, is, with almost every person, the weakest of all. The *pianist*, however, must know how to employ these various degrees of power, so that in playing the scales all the fingers may strike their appropriate keys *with perfect equality of strength;* for the scales sound well only when they are played in every respect *with the most exact equality*.

This equality is *three-fold;* namely—

First. *Equality of strength*.

No one note ought to sound in the smallest degree louder than another, whether it be struck with the thumb, or the first, second, third, or little finger.

Secondly. *Equality in point of quickness*.

Each note must follow the preceding one strictly in the same degree of movement, whether we play the scales slow or quick.

Thirdly and lastly. *Equality in holding the notes down*.

No key must be held down for a longer or shorter time than the rest; that is, each finger must only keep its key pressed down till the following one is struck, and it must then be taken up exactly at the very moment that the next finger comes in contact with its key. This must, of course, also be observed in *passing the thumb under* the middle fingers, or in passing the latter *over* the thumb.

If we offend even against only *one* of these three principal rules, the equality and beauty of the run is destroyed, and the utility of the practice lost. Each scale, therefore, must be practised in the order prescribed in my Pianoforte School, first with the right hand only, and then with both hands, and, *at first, extremely slow*, always consulting the judgment of your teacher, or taking the counsel of your own good ear as to whether the fingers sufficiently observe all the rules.

From week to week you must increase the degree of rapidity, till at last all the fingers are in a condition to fly over the keys with lightness, firmness, and distinct and beautiful execution. Every day, when you seat yourself at the pianoforte, let the *scales* be, for one half hour, the first thing which you attack; as by this means the fingers will be got in readiness for every thing else.

But I will not torment you longer to-day, for I hope soon again to receive intelligence of your further progress, and I remain, Miss,

Yours, &c. &c.

LETTER III.

(TWO MONTHS LATER.)

ON TIME, SUBDIVISION OF THE NOTES, AND
FINGERING.

My dear Miss,

The intelligence of your further progress rejoiced me very much.

Your fingers already begin to develop a well-regulated flexibility; your touch and execution are no longer heavy and sluggish; the finger-exercises, the runs, and scale-passages go off tolerably quick, light, and equal; and, lastly, you already play several dozen little pieces without faults, and generally without stumbling. You see, Miss, that a reasonable degree of diligence and obedience to the precepts of your teacher will soon be rewarded by the most pleasing results.

The difficulty which the observance of the ♯, ♭, ♮, ×, and ♭♭ still causes you, will soon disappear, if you firmly apply your memory to this point, and if you constantly take good notice of, and learn to quickly retain the marks of transposition which are indicated at the beginning of each piece, as well as those which occur accidentally in the bar.

But the time and the *subdivision of the notes* cause you, as you write to me, still much trouble; and we will therefore treat a little on this subject to day.

The *subdivision of the notes* in music is a thing so certain and so positively determined, that we cannot well commit a fault against it, *if we give to each note and rest its exact value, and if, in so doing, we consult the eye rather than the ear.* For the eye always sees aright when it is supported by the memory; but the ear by itself may very often be deceived, particularly in beginners.

The duration of the notes is, as you know, expressed by the fingers being *held down* on the keys; that of the rests, on the contrary, by the fingers *being kept off the keys, and free;* and we must take care not to confound these two things; for each note must be held exactly as long as its prescribed value requires, and the key must not be quitted either sooner or later. Simple and easy as this rule appears, it is often sinned against by much better players than yourself. This arises from the circumstance that most persons are neglectful on this head, when they are first taught; partly out of carelessness, and partly also because the holding down of

At the first decyphering of a new musical piece, the beginner cannot of course easily play in time; since he must bestow great attention on *taking the notes correctly*, and on the fingering, and must stop at each wrong-taken key to set himself right. As soon, however, as this is amended, he must endeavour to play through the piece; at first slowly indeed, and then continue to practise it, till he can go through it as quickly as the composer has indicated.

If you can accustom yourself, while playing, to count *aloud*, it will be exceedingly advantageous to you. But this it is difficult to manage, because, by so doing, freedom of playing is apt to be impeded; and, besides, we easily fall into the error of *counting unequally*. When you practise alone, therefore, it will be best only to *count in idea*, and to consult your ear with great attention, in order to recall to your mind how the piece sounded while your teacher was present. Beating the time with the foot cannot well be recommended, because it often settles into a bad habit.

When long rests occur in both hands, counting mentally or aloud is exceedingly necessary; for you know that, in every musical composition, each bar must occupy exactly the same quantity of time as the rest, whether it consists of notes or rests.

Hitherto, I have only spoken of that sort

of keeping time in which we neither come to a stand-still, nor omit, nor pass over any thing. But there is another sort of keeping time, in which we may observe all this very correctly, and yet commit errors against time.

These faults consist in this—that, in the course of the piece, we either continually play *quicker and quicker* or *slower and slower;* or else, that we sometimes play too quick, and then again too slow.

Into the error of *accelerating* the time, just such young and lively persons as my dear Miss Cecilia are most apt to fall; and who knows whether I have not guessed right when I imagine that you sometimes begin a piece which goes off pretty fluently, at first very quietly and sagely; but then, becoming excited as you go on, you play quicker and quicker, and at last, finish with such rapidity as if your fingers were holding a run-away pony? Have I not guessed right?

To avoid this, you must practise even those pieces *which you already play well*, as composedly and as attentively as when you first began to study them; and in so doing, you must not allow the fingers to indulge their own fancies, or to be in the least degree inattentive. For the fingers are little disobedient creatures, if they are not kept well-reined in; and they are apt to run off like an unbroken colt as soon as they have gained some degree of fluency.

The opposite fault of *hanging back*, or dragging in the time, generally proceeds from our having begun too fast; and by that means stumbling against difficulties which we cannot overcome in that quick degree of movement.

Hence this capital rule: *never begin a piece quicker than you can with certainty go on with it to the very end.*

There are exceptions to this rule, which you will be taught by and by, when you learn the higher branches of expression and execution.

You will already have remarked, how necessary correct fingering is in playing. A single ill-chosen finger may often cause the complete failure of a whole passage, or, at least, make it sound coarse, unequal, and disagreeable. As doubtless you have studied all the elementary pieces exactly with fingering indicated, your fingers are, to a certain degree, already accustomed to a regular system of fingering. But as, in other compositions, you may, by and by, be often in doubt on this head —before you proceed to the Second Part of this Pianoforte School, which treats of fingering—I will impart, by the way, a few rules on this subject, as to what must be *observed* or *avoided* in every regular system of fingering.

First. When several keys are to be played one after another, either in ascending or in descending, and that five fingers are not sufficient for this purpose, the four longer fingers must never be turned over one another; but we must either pass the thumb *under*, or pass the three middle fingers *over* the thumb.

Secondly. The thumb must never be placed on the black keys.

Thirdly. We must not strike two or more keys one after another with the self-same finger; for each key must always retain its own finger.

Fourthly. In runs, the little finger should never be placed on the black keys.

Fifthly. In chords and wide extensions, however, the thumb, as well as the little finger, may occasionally fall upon the black keys.

Sixthly. The fingering given for the *scales* must be resorted to everywhere, and as much as possible.

Seventhly. At each note that we strike, we must consider whether, for the following notes, the appropriate fingers stand in readiness.

In general, that mode of fingering must be chosen by which we may most easily and naturally be able to maintain a tranquil and fine position of the hands, a firm and perpendicular percussion, as well as a correct holding down of the keys, and a beautiful and connected performance of the melody and of the scales and runs.

I am so convinced that an exact observance of what I have hitherto laid down will, in a short time, enable you to conquer all elementary difficulties, that I trust, in my next intelligence from you, to receive the assurance of this being the case: and, in this pleasing anticipation, I remain,

&c. &c.

LETTER IV.

(THREE MONTHS LATER.)

ON EXPRESSION, AND GRACES OR EMBELLISHMENTS.

HAVE I not already told you, my industrious little girl, that the zealous practice of all the finger-exercises, and the quickly studying of a good many musical pieces, would soon bring you very forward? You write to me that your fingers have already acquired very considerable facility and certainty; that you now begin to study pieces of more importance, development, and difficulty; that you are already able to play, at sight, many short, easy movements, intelligibly and without stopping; and that even keys, with a good many sharps or flats, do not easily confuse you. Allow me, Miss, to assure you that I did not expect less from your industry and talent, and from the well-directed endeavours of your very respectable teacher.

You are now arrived at the epoch where the art begins to proffer you true, noble, and intellectual pleasures, and in which the new and continually more and more beautiful compositions, with which you will now become acquainted, will give you an idea of the inexhaustible riches and variety in music.

But, Miss, do not neglect to still continue practising, with equal or even greater zeal, the finger-exercises, and especially the scales in all the keys.

The utility of this accessory practice is infinite; and, in particular, the diatonic and chromatic scales possess peculiar properties, which even the most skilful players have yet to fathom.

I also request you most earnestly, while you are studying new pieces, not by any means to forget those already learned, not even the earliest ones.

New pieces serve but little, if, on their account, the preceding ones are forgotten.

For the adroitness and expertness of the fingers, the eyes, and the ears must of necessity repose firmly and fundamentally on the experience which we have already gained; while these qualities are to be enlarged and refined by new acquisitions. If, for example, you forget a piece which it took you three weeks to learn, these three weeks are as good as lost. You should therefore retain, as a sort of absolute property, all the pieces you have ever learned; keep them safely, and never lend or give them away.

"Yes," say you, "if it did not take up so much time to continue practising what I have already learned, and also to study new pieces." Dear Miss, you cannot imagine what may be effected, in one single day, if we *properly avail ourselves of the time.*

If, with a fixed determination to excel on the pianoforte, you dedicate to it, *daily, only three hours,* of which about half an hour shall be appropriated to the exercises, as much more to playing over the old pieces, and the remaining time to the study of new compositions,—this will assuredly enable you, by degrees, to attain a very commanding degree of excellence, without necessarily obliging you to neglect your other pursuits.

Your instructor has already accustomed you to observe, in general, the marks of expression; as *forte, piano, legato, staccato, &c.* The more you begin to overcome all the mechanical difficulties of pianoforte-playing, the greater the attention you must give to this important subject—*expression.*

Expression, feeling, and sensibility are the soul of music, as of every other art. If we were to play a piece of music with exactly the same degree of forte or piano throughout, it would sound as ridiculous, as if we were to recite a beautiful poem in the same monotonous tone with which we are used to repeat the multiplication table.

In every composition, the marks of expression, *f. p. cres. dim, legato, staccato, acceler. ritard. &c.* are so exactly indicated by the composer, that the performer can never be in doubt where he is to play loud or soft, increasing or decreasing as to tone, connected or detached, hurrying onwards in the time, or holding it back.

The same exactitude with which you are obliged to observe the notes, the marks of transposition, the fingering, and the time, you must likewise employ with regard to the marks of expression.

But the most difficult part of the business is, *always to observe the proper medium* at each mark of expression; for you already know that there is great diversity in the shades and degrees of forte, piano, legato, staccato, accelerando, and ritardando.

The utmost fortissimo should never degenerate into mere hammering and thumping, or into maltreating the instrument.

Similarly, the most gentle pianissimo ought never to become indistinct and unintelligible.

You possess an excellent pianoforte by one of our best makers; and you will already have remarked, that the most gentle pressure of the finger on a key produces a perceptible alteration and modification in the tone; and that we may play with great power, without any excessive exertion, and without using any unnecessary and ridiculous movements of the hands, arms, shoulders, or head. For, unhappily, many even very good pianists are guilty of these and similar contortions and grimaces; against which, my dear girl, I must warn you.

Many, too, have the detestable habit, when they wish to strike a note with peculiar emphasis, of elevating their knuckles so much, that the hand seems to form waves, like troubled waters.

Others endeavour to manifest their feelings by widely jerking out their elbows; or they mark the commencement of every bar by making a low bow with their head and chest, as if they were desirous of shewing reverence to their own playing. Others, after every short note, suddenly take up their hands as far from the keys as if they had touched a red hot iron. Many, while playing, put on a fierce and crabbed countenance; others, again, assume a perpetual simper, &c. One of the worst faults is carrying to excess the ritardando and accelerando, so that we are often several minutes without knowing whether the piece is written in triple or in common time. This produces nearly the same effect as if some one were addressing us in a strange and unintelligible language.

To all these faults, we may accustom ourselves, in the zeal of practice, *without knowing it;* and when, to our mortification, we are made to observe them, it is often too late wholly to leave them off.

Do not suppose, however, that you are to sit at the piano as stiff and cold as a wooden doll. Some graceful movements are *necessary* while playing; it is only the *excess* that must be avoided.

When we have to play in the highest or lowest octave, a gentle inclination of the body is at once necessary and appropriate. When we have to play difficult passages, chords struck loud and short, or skips, the hands are and must be allowed a moderate degree of movement. As we must sometimes look at the notes, and sometimes at the hands, a slight movement of the head is, if not necessary, at least very excusable. Still, however, you should accustom yourself to look rather at the notes than at the fingers.

But the elegant deportment of polished life must always be transferred to the art; and the rule applies, generally, " that every movement which conduces really and essentially to our better playing is allowed;" here, however, we must avoid all that is unnecessary and superfluous.

At present it would be too early to direct your attention to certain more refined rules of expression. In the mean time, 1 beg of you to observe, in the strictest manner, all that each composer has indicated on this head in his works; and to try to execute each piece in a pure and flowing manner, and in the time indicated by the author. Towards effecting this last object, Maelzel's metronome will afford you very great assistance in most modern compositions.

The *graces*, namely, the shake, the turn, the appoggiatura, &c. are the flowers of music; and the clear, correct, and delicate execution of them, embellishes and exalts every melody and every passage. But, when they are played stiff, hard, or unintelligibly, they may rather be compared to blots of ink or spots of dirt.

The shake is peculiarly important; and, to a pianist, the elegant, equal, and rapid execution of it, is as much an ornament and a duty as the equal and pearly execution of the scales. In the right hand, at least, it ought to be played alike well *with all the fingers*. The equality of the shake can only be attained by lifting up both fingers to an *equal height*, and striking the keys with equal force. You ought to devote a few minutes daily to this particular practice. The examples necessary for the purpose you will find in the Pianoforte School, as well as in many pieces.

Therefore, Miss, continue firm in your present diligent course, and reckon always on the best-meant counsel from

Yours, &c. &c.

LETTER V.

(TWO MONTHS LATER.)

ON THE KEYS, ON STUDYING A PIECE, AND ON PLAYING IN THE PRESENCE OF OTHERS.

You are now well acquainted with all the twenty-four keys, and with the scales and chords belonging to them; and it is with pleasure I learn that you even now daily play through all the scales and passages in them, as diligently as you formerly did those in the twelve major keys; and that you acknowledge the many advantages of these exercises, by which also you save yourself the labour of wading through so many tedious *études*, or professed studies.

One of the most necessary acquirements for a pianist is to be *equally practised and ready in all the keys.* There are many who are as much startled at a piece having four or five sharps or flats for its signature, as though they saw a spectre. And, nevertheless, to the *fingers* all keys are in reality of equal difficulty; for there are as difficult compositions in C major as in C sharp major. Only that the *eye* and the *memory* must be early accustomed to this great number of marks of transposition.

As, in such unusual keys, the black keys must be principally employed, and as they are narrower than the white ones, and therefore less certain as to the striking of them; it is absolutely requisite on the part of the player, that he should keep his hand particularly firm, and somewhat higher than usual over the keys, and employ a very decided touch, in order to acquire the same degree of certainty as on the white keys.

You complain, Miss, that the studying of difficult pieces still costs you much time and labour. There is a certain remedy against this, which I may call the *art of studying*, and which I will impart to you, as far as it can be done in writing.

There are pupils who study such compositions attentively enough it is true, but so slow and with such frequent interruptions, that these pieces become tedious and disagreeable to them before they have half learned them. Such pupils often take half a year to learn a few pieces tolerably; and, by this wasteful expenditure of time, always remain in the back-ground.

Others, on the contrary, try to conquer every thing by force; and imagine that they shall succeed in this by practising for hours, laboriously indeed, but in an inattentive and thoughtless manner, and by hastily playing over all kinds of difficulties innumerable times. These persons play till their fingers are lamed; but how? confusedly, over hastily, and without expression; or, what is still worse, *with a false expression*.

We may escape all this by keeping the right medium between these two ways. When, therefore, you begin to learn a new and somewhat difficult piece, you must devote the first hours to decyphering the notes strictly and correctly in a slow time. You must also fix upon the fingering to be employed, and gain a general insight over the whole. This, in a single piece, can at most require but a few days. Then the whole piece must be played over quietly and composedly, but at the same time attentively, and without any distraction of ideas, till we are enabled to execute it without trouble, and in the exact time indicated by the author.

Single passages of great difficulty may be practised apart. Still, however, they ought to be often repeated in connection with the rest of the piece.

All this too may be completed in a few days. But now begins the time when we must also learn to *play it with beauty and elegance*.

Now, all the marks of expression must be observed with redoubled attention; and we must endeavour to seize correctly on the character of the composition, and to enforce it in our performance according to its total effect.

To this belongs the very important quality, *that the player should know how to listen properly to himself, and to judge of his own performance with accuracy.* He who does not possess this gift, is apt, in practising alone, to spoil all that he has acquired correctly in the presence of his teacher.

But I must once more remind you, Miss, that we can only study new pieces quickly and well, when we have not forgotten those already learned. There are, alas! many pupils (female pupils too, dear Miss) who play only that piece well which they have just been taught. All those acquired before are neglected and thrown aside. Such pupils will never make any great progress. For you must own, Miss, that those persons who play fifty pieces well, are much more clever than those who, like a bird-organ, can only play two or three pieces in a tolerable manner: and that the first, by a proper employment of our time, is very possible, I believe I have already said to you.

Your worthy teacher has acted very properly in early accustoming you to play occasionally before others. At first, this, as you write to me, was very disagreeable to you, and you felt much frightened in so doing. "But now," say you, " I think nothing of it ; nay, it generally gives me great pleasure, particularly when all goes off well." And there you are quite right. To what purpose do we learn, but to give pleasure, not only to ourselves, but also to our beloved parents and our worthy friends ? And assuredly there is no higher satisfaction than in being able to distinguish oneself before a large company, and in receiving an honorable acknowledgment of one's diligence and talent.

But to bring matters to this point, we must be thoroughly sure of our business; for want of success is, on the contrary, as vexatious as tormenting and disgraceful. Above all, you must select, for this purpose, such compositions as are fully within your powers, and respecting the good effect of which you can entertain no doubt. Every difficult piece becomes doubly difficult when we play it before others, because the natural diffidence of the performer impedes the free development of his abilities.

Many half-formed players imagine that every thing will be right, if they do but step forward at once with a difficult piece by some celebrated composer. But by this means they neither do honor to the composition nor to themselves; but merely expose themselves to the danger of exciting ennui, and, at best, of being applauded from politeness and compassion, and therefore of being blamed and laughed at behind their backs. For, even with regard to amateurs, persons avail themselves of the right to blame when they have not received any pleasure; and, in fact, who can take their doing so in bad part?

Many, otherwise very good players, have in this manner, by an unsuitable choice of pieces, lost both their musical reputation and all future confidence in themselves.

When playing before others, you should particularly endeavour to execute your *well-studied* piece with tranquillity and self-possession, without hurrying, without allowing your ideas to wander, and *more especially without coming to a stand-still;* for this last is the most unpleasant fault which we can commit before an audience.

Before you commence, the fingers must be kept quite warm; you must avoid any inconvenient mode of dress; and you should, if possible, always play on a pianoforte with which you are well acquainted; for an instrument, of which the touch is much lighter or much heavier than that which one is accustomed to, may very much confuse a player.

But, besides professedly playing before others, it may often happen that you are suddenly required, in the company of intimate acquaintance, to play over some trifle to them.

It is very necessary, therefore, Miss, that you should study and commit to memory a good number of little, easy, but tasteful pieces; so that, on such occasions, you may be able to play them *by heart:* for it appears rather childish to be obliged, for every trifle, to turn over one's collection of music; or, when in a strange place, to be always obliged to draw back, with the excuse " that you cannot play any thing by heart."

I would lay a wager, Miss Cecilia, that you have been so situated; is it not so ?

For this purpose, short rondos, pretty airs with variations, melodies from operas, nay, even dance-tunes, waltzes, quadrilles, marches, &c. &c. are perfectly suitable; for *every thing does credit to the player which is well played.*

As it is very proper to let a little prelude precede any musical composition, you must have by heart a number of this sort of pieces, in all the keys. You will find the means necessary for so doing in my Pianoforte School, as well as in many collections of such preludes.

The playing before others has also the great advantage, that it compels one to study with unusual zeal. For the idea that we must play before an audience, spurs us on to a much greater measure of diligence than if we play only to ourselves, or to the four senseless walls.

I shall therefore close this letter, Miss, with the request that you will not neglect any proper occasion of exhibiting your fine talent to the world; and I remain,

&c. &c.

LETTER VI.

ON THE SELECTION OF COMPOSITIONS MOST SUITABLE
FOR EACH PIANIST.

You wish to know, Miss, what compositions you are chiefly to play, so that you may learn all that are good, as far as that is possible, and that too in a natural and progressive order; and it does credit to your taste, that you are desirous not only of studying the favorite pieces of the present day, but likewise the most striking works of the earlier and more ancient masters.

Your worthy teacher has already recommended to you the admirable Studies of Bertini, Cramer, &c. as also the excellent Grand Scale-Exercises of Clementi; and I cannot but rejoice that you have also had the goodness and patience to occupy yourself with some of my own contributions towards furthering volubility of execution,—such as my School for Virtuosi; —of Graces and embellishments;—of Legato and Staccato, &c.

The studies just named have, for the greater part, a merely practical aim; but, in the present day, there frequently appears, under the same titles, grand and difficult pieces by Chopin, Hiller, Hummel, Henselt, Kalkbrenner, Liszt, Potter, Thalberg, and many others, which I shall recommend you to study at some future time, when your execution shall have reached a very high degree of excellence: for most of these pieces are splendid bravura-compositions, intended rather for highly cultivated players, and for public performances, than for the instruction of those who, like you, Miss, have still to climb many steps to arrive at perfection.

Useful as these studies are in general, we must not lose sight of the fact, that *every* piece, be it a sonata, a rondo, an air with variations, a fantasia, &c. is also a *study* in its way; and that, for example, we may draw from a concerto, or a set of brilliant variations, equally as much advantage in regard to rapidity of finger, or from a sentimental adagio equally as much improvement in regard to expression, as we can from the practice of any set of studies whatever.

The authors which you have chiefly studied as yet, were well adapted to the purpose; for, at first, pupils require such compositions as combine pleasing and intelligible melody, and modern taste, with passages naturally calculated for preserving a fine position of the hands; as, for example, the *easier* works of *Bertini, Herz, Hünten, Kalkbrenner, Moscheles, &c. &c.*

But you have now arrived at an epoch when the *more difficult works* of the above-named masters, as also of *Hummel, Cramer, Dussek, Ries, Steibelt*, and the easier ones of *Beethoven*, are very suitable and proper for you.

In the course of the ensuing year, with the same industry and zeal, you may easily arrive at that degree of advancement, that you will be enabled to study by yourself, and with the best results, the difficult works of the present as well as of past times; such as those of *Chopin, Thalberg, Liszt, Field*, &c. as also the Concertos of *Hummel, Kalkbrenner*, and *Moscheles;* and, lastly, the best compositions of *Mozart, Clementi, Beethoven, Cramer, Dussek, Prince Louis Ferdinand of Prussia*, &c.

In the choice of musical pieces, we should always bear in mind the following points:

1st. That we ought always to proceed from the more easy to the more difficult as to execution.

2ndly. That, as far as possible, we should make ourselves acquainted with the works of *all* the great composers, and not by any means tie ourselves down to any favorite author.

3rdly. That, by degrees, we should also thoroughly learn the classical and truly valuable works of the earlier composers.

Every distinguished composer requires to

be played in a style peculiar to himself. With many, there predominates a brilliant, showy, and strongly marked manner; with others, an expressive, quiet, connected, and gentle style of playing is most generally called for; others, again, require a characteristic, impassioned, or even fantastic and humorous expression; and, in many compositions, a tender, warm, playful, and pleasing mode of execution is most suitable. Lastly, there are pieces which include all these different styles, and which therefore compel the player to adopt corresponding alternations of manner in his performance. Thus, for example, *Hummel's* compositions require an extraordinary and pearl-like mode of execution, which is produced by a lightly *dropping* of the keys, as I have explained to you in my Pianoforte School. In *Beethoven's* works this style will seldom be suitable; as, in them, great characteristic energy, deep feeling, often capricious humor, and a sometimes very legato, and at others a very marked and emphatic style of playing are requisite.

A piece which is played too fast or too slow loses all its effect, and becomes quite disfigured. Where the time is not marked according to Maelzel's metronome, the player must look to the Italian words which indicate the degree of movement; as *allegro, moderato, presto*, &c. and likewise to the character of the composition, and gradually learn by experience to know their real significations.

No less important is the proper mode of treating the *pedals;* and I beg of you, Miss, to observe strictly all that I have said on this subject in my Pianoforte School.

By a proper employment of the forte or damper pedal, the player is enabled to produce effects which would seem to require that he should have two pair of hands at his command. But, used at an improper time, this pedal causes an unpleasant and unintelligible noise, which falls on the ear as disagreeably as a writing on wet paper falls on the eye.

I have already explained how important to the pupil is a gradual and easy progression, as to difficulty, in the selection of pieces intended for him; and I shall now add a few words more on this head. Every composer, as well as every player, founds his art and his science on what his *predecessors* have already done; adding to that the inventions of his own talent. By these natural steps in advance, it is evident that the compositions of the present distinguished pianists are in many respects much more difficult than those of times gone by; and that whoever desires to study them must already possess great knowledge of music, and a very considerable degree of execution.

Many pupils, however, as soon as their fingers have acquired some little facility, and led astray by the charms of novelty, run into the error of attacking the most difficult compositions. Not a few who can hardly play the scales in a decent manner, and who ought to practise for years *studies* and easy and appropriate pieces, have the presumption to attempt *Hummel's concertos* or *Thalberg's fantasias!*

The natural result of this over-haste, is, that such players, by omitting the requisite preparatory studies, always continue imperfect, lose much time, and are at last unable to execute either difficult or easy pieces in a creditable manner.

This is the true cause why, although so many talented young folks devote themselves to the pianoforte, we are still not so over and above rich in good players, as, beyond all doubt, was the case formerly; and why so many, with the best dispositions, and often with enormous industry, still remain but mediocre and indifferent performers.

Many other pupils run into the error of attempting to decide on the merits of a composition before they are able to play it properly. From this it happens that many excellent pieces appear contemptible to them, while the fault lies in their playing them in a stumbling, incorrect, and unconnected manner, often coming to a stand-still on false and discordant harmonies, missing the time, &c. &c.

You have, no doubt, Miss, frequently been placed in this situation; and I would wager that you have sometimes impatiently thrown aside a piece which did not much promise to please you. In this manner, you must, in the sequel, have often lost that exquisite enjoyment which the ingenious and elaborate works of the great masters offer to you, if you have the patience to overcome the difficulties generally inseparable from them.

Here more particularly belong compositions in what is called the *strict style*; as, for example, the works of Handel, Bach, and other masters of this stamp. For the execution of such pieces, generally written in several parts, and in the *fugue* style, and of such single passages in the same style as we often meet with in the most modern compositions, there are required a strict *legato*, and a very firm and equal touch; and also a clear enunciation of each single part; and, for the attainment of all this, the employment of a peculiar mode of fingering, which, in general, deviates very much from the usual one, and which chiefly consists in quickly and adroitly substituting one finger for another on the same key, while it is held down, and without sounding it anew.

By this substitution, the five fingers are in a manner multiplied *ad infinitum*, and we are enabled to play each of the four parts, of which such passages in general consist, as smoothly, connectedly, and in as singing a manner as though we had so many hands.

I beg you, Miss, to study very attentively all that I have said on these subjects in the Second and Third Parts of my Pianoforte School, and to retain it equally in your memory and at your fingers' ends.

I have now once more put your patience to the test. But I beg of you to recollect, Miss, that much of what I now write to you is calculated for a future period; and therefore that reading over these remarks by and by will prove of still more particular service to you.

In the mean while, I subscribe myself,
&c. &c.

LETTER VII.

(SOME MONTHS LATER.)

RUDIMENTS OF THOROUGH-BASS.

It is with great pleasure that I now fulfil the desire which you expressed that I would give you some preliminary notion of Harmony or Thorough-bass, to facilitate the study of it, when you, by and by, commence with your worthy teacher this very necessary and interesting science on a more extended scale.

First of all, I will endeavour, by the following explanations, to give you as clear an idea as possible of what thorough-bass or harmony is, and to what purpose it serves.

Music consists of *melody* and *harmony*. When, for example, a female sings quite alone, without any accompaniment, her song is pure, simple melody. When another female singer, with a somewhat deeper voice, accompanies the first with a different, but still agreeably sounding melody, this will form music in *two parts*, which may also be called two-part harmony.

When to these two voices a third person, with a high male voice, adds his accompaniment, there arises a harmony in *three parts.*

Lastly, imagine a deep male or *bass voice*, by way of accompaniment, and we shall have a harmony in *four parts*, in which each part sings a different melody, and nevertheless the whole together sounds harmonious and pleasing to the ear. You will easily imagine, Miss, that the three singers who accompany the first do not sing at hazard, and merely what may strike them; for this would produce a horrible discordance: consequently the chords of which this four-part harmony consists, are arranged by the composer according to certain rules, in order to produce that fine effect.

Those rules are just what we are taught to know by thorough-bass; and consequently the theory of harmony consists in shewing—

1st. *What chords are possible in music;* and,

2nd. *How these chords must succeed each other in a regular manner, so as to give to each melody the necessary harmonic ground-work, or accompaniment.*

" But," you will ask, " in the pieces which I play, whole lines often occur, in which there are no chords, and nothing but running or skipping passages in one hand, while the other strikes single notes; or there are passages in both hands. Does all this too arise from thorough-bass?"

Exactly so, Miss; for all these passages are nothing but varied or arpeggioed chords: and, in all music, no bar occurs which does not repose on this foundation.

Even the fullest chords, which often consist of ten, nay, even of twenty or thirty notes, are for the most part formed from four essential, that is, really different notes. The rest are only *duplications* of them.

If we consider the following example in four parts,

and afterwards this,

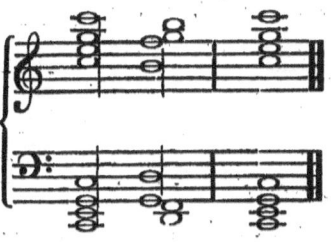

we shall readily perceive that the second example is only an extended duplication of the first, that it consists of the same chords, and consequently contains only four *real* parts.

We shall now give some examples in which these chords are varied and broken into arpeggios.

We can, as you see, form from these chords innumerable passages, and even entire melodies, while the harmony on which they are founded always remains the same. And it is the same with all the other chords which are practicable in music.

A composer must have studied thorough-bass well; as otherwise he would, in every composition, entangle himself in irregular, and therefore irresoluble, discords. And, even to the *player* and *practical musician*, this science ought not to remain unknown; for it is equally useful and pleasant to be able to account to oneself, as to how far each composition may justly lay claim to intrinsic merit; and because thorough-bass is of the greatest assistance in *extemporizing*, *playing at sight*, and *accompanying*.

But before we learn to know the chords, we must see *from what* they are constructed.

Each chord must consist of at least three notes, sounded together. When we strike only two notes together, it is not a chord, but merely an *interval*.

There are *ten* such intervals in music, which here follow; C being always taken as the lower note or root.

Unison.　Second.　Third.　Fourth.　Fifth.

With respect to these intervals, the following remarks are to be made:

1st. Any key which we choose to fix upon, may serve as a root or bottom note to all these intervals; and consequently they may take place in all keys and in all octaves.

2ndly. They receive their names from the greater or less distance from their root, and that according to the number of degrees by which they are removed from it. Thus, for example, the third is distant three degrees of the diatonic scale from the lower note or root; the fifth, five degrees; the sixth, six degrees; and so on.

3rdly. The unison (or like sound) is no interval; but it must be so considered in thorough-bass, because two different parts occasionally take one and the same note.

4thly. When we strike intervals separated by still wider distances than the tenth,—as, for example,

such intervals are merely fourths, fifths, sixths,

sevenths, &c. taken one or more octaves higher; and even the most remote distances, extending through all the octaves, make no difference in this respect. Even the tenth is nothing but a third taken an octave higher.

5thly. The ninth is also, in truth, but a second taken an octave higher; but, in thorough-bass, it is used in a different manner in both forms; and it is therefore named sometimes in the one way, sometimes in the other.

6thly. All intervals are computed and sought for from the lower note *upwards,*—that is, in the direction from the bass towards the treble,—and never in the reverse way, or from the upper note downwards. Their *inversions* will be explained afterwards.

7thly. The above scheme of intervals I have written on C as a root, and therefore in the key of C major; and, as I proceed, I shall also give all the subsequent examples in one key only, generally that of C major or A minor.

It is, however, of the greatest importance that you should transpose all these examples into all the other keys, and that too in *writing;* for which purpose, your having learned to copy music will be very useful. It is to be remembered here, that all the examples in a major key can only be transposed into major keys; and, similarly, all the examples in minor, only into minor keys. Thus, as the preceding scheme of intervals is formed from the diatonic scale of C major, it can only be written in this way in all the rest of the major keys; and the key-note of the scale selected must always be taken as the root from which all the intervals must be sought for in ascending.

By way of illustration, I shall give you a similar diagram in A♭ major.

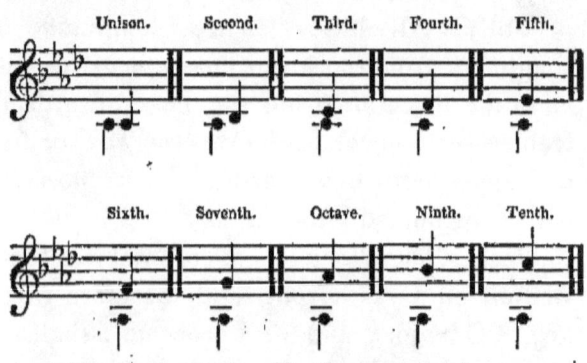

And similarly in all other major keys.

You know, Miss, that every note may be raised or depressed by means of the ♯, ♭, ♮, ×, ♭♭. And as this is naturally possible also with respect to every interval, each of them admits of *three*, or even *four* different kinds; and this difference is indicated and determined by the epithets, *diminished, minor* (or *false*), *major* (or *perfect*), and *superfluous*, as may be seen in the following table:

The tenth is the same as the third.

You will observe, Miss, that many different intervals, when struck, are taken on the very same keys. For example, the superfluous second and the minor third; or the superfluous fourth and the false fifth, &c.

But, in thorough-bass, these intervals are distinguished from one another in two ways:

1st. Because each of them requires, for its

accompaniments, quite different notes, which therefore form quite different chords; and

2ndly. Because each is resolved in quite another manner. You will shortly learn this difference more fully.

You will also have further remarked, that, in each species of interval, the notes retain the same alphabetical names, whether it is minor, major, or superfluous; the difference is produced merely by the marks of transposition, whether ♯ or ♭.

Here follows the same scheme of intervals in two more keys.

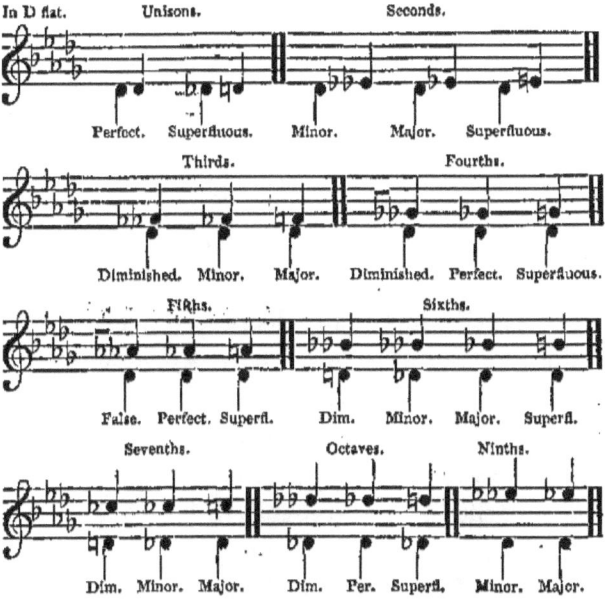

In the last example you will observe, with regard to the diminished sixth and diminished seventh, that these two intervals in D♭ cannot be produced in any other manner than by *raising the bottom note* or *root*.

In transposing these examples, you must observe this in each key, whenever, owing to the too great number of sharps or flats, these intervals cannot be produced in any other manner.

And now, Miss, I leave it to your diligence to impress all this thoroughly on your mind, by writing it and committing it to memory; and in our next we shall occupy ourselves with the formation of chords.

LETTER VIII.

ON THE FORMATION OF CHORDS.

You will already have discovered, Miss, that, among intervals, many sound agreeably, and many others very much the reverse. For this reason, intervals are divided into such as are *consonant* (or agreeable to the ear), and *dissonant* (or disagreeable to the ear).

Consonant intervals are :
(*a.*) The perfect unison ;
(*b.*) The major and minor third ;
(*c.*) The perfect fifth ;
(*d.*) The major and minor sixth ;
(*e.*) The perfect octave ;
(*f.*) The major and minor tenth.
All others are dissonant.

Consonant intervals are still further divided into *perfect* and *imperfect*.

The perfect are : the perfect fifth and perfect octave.

The imperfect are : the major and minor third, and the major and minor sixth.

Concords are distinguished from discords, among other properties, by the latter requiring a *resolution*; that is to say, that the dissonant interval must be resolved into a consonant one; and this resolution must therefore naturally at last take place on a concord.

Among all the chords practicable in music, there is only one in each key which is called the *perfect common chord*, or *perfect triad*. It consists of a bass note or root, its third, its fifth, and when in four parts, the perfect octave also: viz.

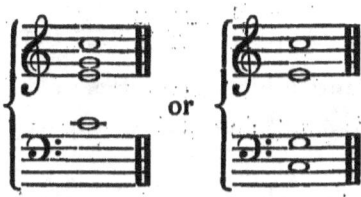

The third may be either major or minor, according as the key is major or minor; but the fifth and octave must be perfect.

I must once more remind you that all the intervals in each chord are always computed and sought for from the *lowest* note upwards.

In the two preceding examples the octave is the highest part. But as the third or the fifth may also be the highest part, it follows that the perfect common chord admits of *three positions*, which are named according to the interval which occurs at the top or highest part. Ex.

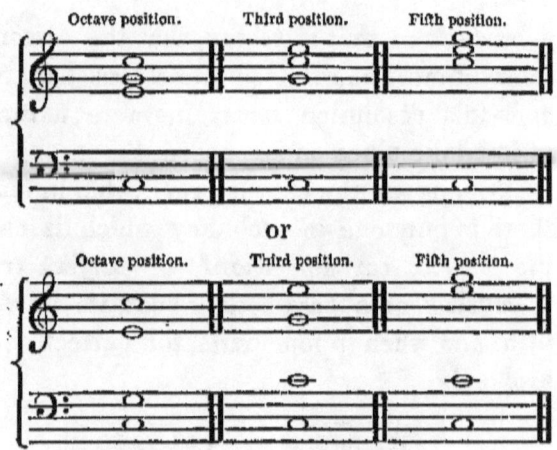

For the different changes or duplications of the *middle parts* do not, in any way, change the chord.

All this also occurs in the minor mode; that is, when the minor third is taken in place of the major third.

But the perfect common chord admits also of two *inversions*, by which two less perfect, though still consonant chords originate.

The inversion of a chord occurs when the bass, instead of the root, takes one of the other notes of which the chord consists. For example,

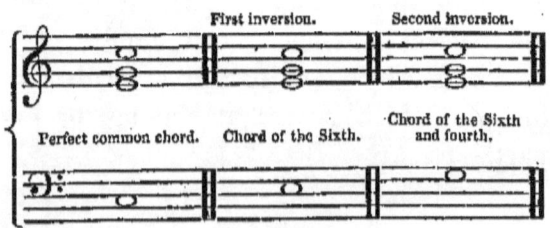

The chord of the sixth, so called because its principal interval is the sixth, has also its three positions, like the perfect common chord. Example:

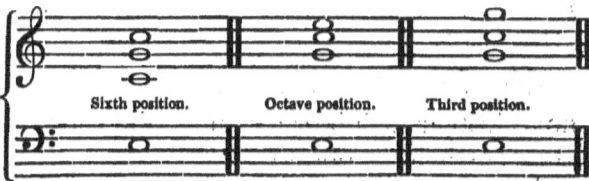

Just so it is with the chord of the sixth and fourth, which derives its name from its containing those intervals. Ex.

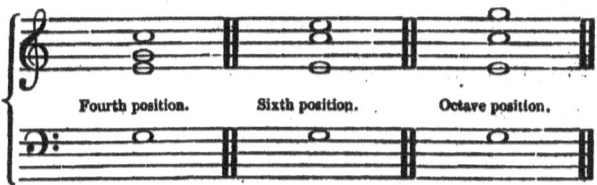

It is very necessary to know all these chords readily in their different forms.

All this equally applies to minor keys, if, instead of E♮, we every where take E♭.

These two chords are less perfect than the common chord, because, although they are tolerably agreeable, they do not sound so satisfactorily as to enable us to make a close or cadence by means of them.

Although the perfect common chord may occur on each degree of the diatonic scale

F

(though, however, on the seventh degree it appears with an imperfect fifth), it is nevertheless most important, when placed on the *first* degree of the key in which we are playing, as it alone can establish and determine the key.

We now come to the second PRINCIPAL CHORD in thorough-bass; namely, the *chord of the minor or dominant seventh.*

It consists of a bass note, its major third, perfect fifth, and minor seventh, and consequently of *four* essential parts; so that it requires no duplication of notes to be in four parts.

It takes place on the fifth degree, or dominant note of every scale; and therefore, in C major or minor, it falls upon G. Ex.

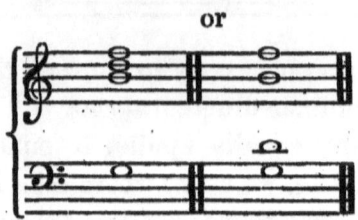

You are already conversant with this chord, from the scale-exercises in my Pianoforte School, where it serves to form the passage or transition from one key to another.

It has the property of requiring a natural,

and to the ear desirable, resolution into the perfect common chord. Ex.

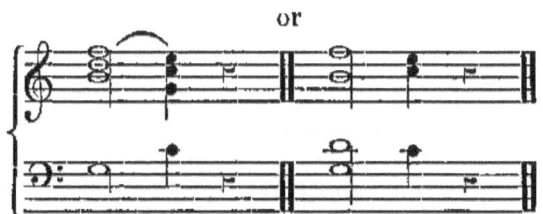

It has four different positions; viz.

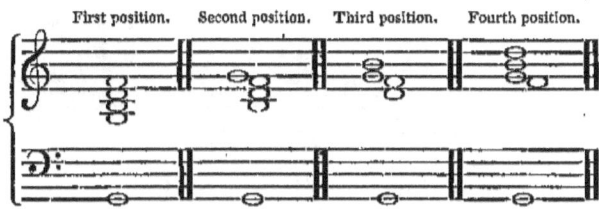

In all these positions, it always remains the same chord of the seventh.

In addition to this, it has also three inversions, by which three different chords originate, namely, the chord of the fifth and sixth, that of the sixth, fourth, and third, and the chord of the second.

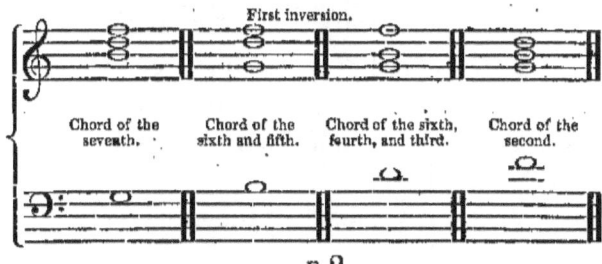

Each of these new chords has also its different positions. Ex.

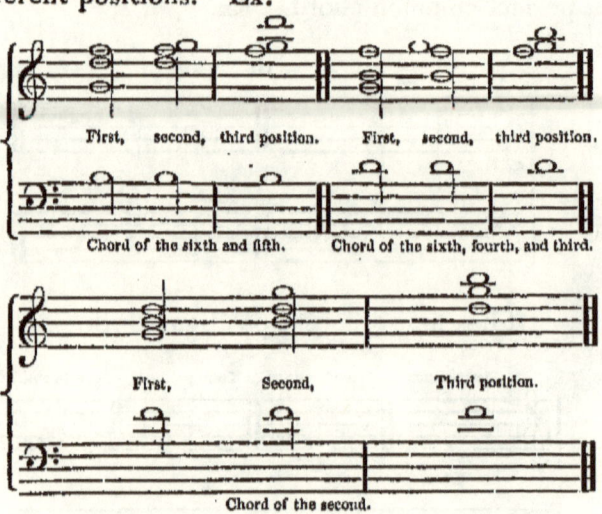

The natural resolution of these chords is also into the perfect common chord. The chord of the second, however, is resolved by one of the inversions of that chord. Ex.

In the chord of the second, you will observe, Miss, that the discord of the second, though rather harsh in itself, sounds pleasingly enough in this application of it.

When the chord of the seventh is played

on other degrees of the scale, it is very dissonant, though still capable of being employed. Ex.

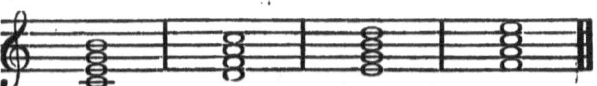

If, in the first of these four chords, we were to make the seventh minor, it would certainly sound much better; but *it would no longer be in C major*, but in F.   Ex.

I have already made you acquainted with seven chords. If you give yourself the trouble to transpose them into the other keys, you will speedily be able to trace them out in every composition, under whatever forms they may occasionally be hidden. We will, in our next, learn the remaining chords; and till then believe me, &c.

LETTER IX.

CONTINUATION OF THOROUGH-BASS.

Dear Miss,

Each interval assists in the formation of some particular chord; and if, therefore, we go through all the intervals in this point of view, you will become tolerably well acquainted with all the chords which can be employed in music.

The PERFECT UNISON is no real interval; but two different parts are often obliged to meet on the very same note, by which means the unison is formed. Ex.

The × shews where the above interval occurs.

The SUPERFLUOUS UNISON is a harsh discord, which is occasionally employed by way of what is termed a *passing note*.

The SECONDS are all discords, and, like all other dissonant combinations, require in general to be *prepared*, as well as *resolved*.

Preparation occurs when we previously take a concord suitable to the purpose.

To the *minor second* there is required, to make it a chord in four parts, the perfect fourth and the minor sixth. Ex.

To the *major second* is required the perfect fourth and the major sixth.

To the *superfluous second* belong the superfluous fourth and the major sixth.

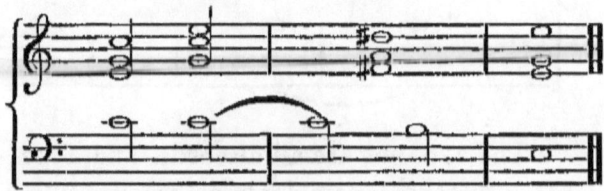

To the *diminished third*, which is a harsh discord, belong the false fifth and the diminished seventh. Ex.

The *minor* and *major third* belong to the perfect common chord, as you know; and these chords we have already become acquainted with.

To the *diminished fourth* is to be added the doubled minor sixth.

To the *perfect fourth* may be added either the perfect fifth, or the major or minor sixth.

To the *superfluous fourth* belong the major second and major sixth, or, in lieu of the second, occasionally the minor third.

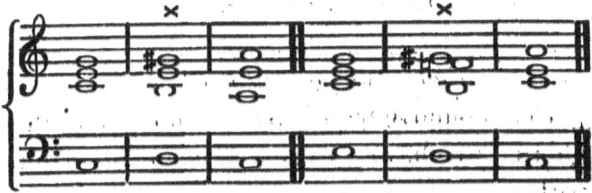

To the *diminished* or *false fifth* is generally added the minor third and minor sixth. It then forms the chord of the sixth and fifth, which we already know.

The *perfect fifth* we know already from the common chord.

To the *superfluous fifth* belong the major third and perfect octave.

The *diminished sixth* is accompanied by the minor third and diminished seventh.

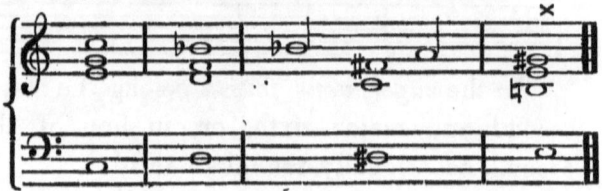

To the *major* and *minor sixth* we usually add the major or minor third and the octave; and we already know this chord as the first inversion of the perfect common chord.

To the *superfluous sixth* belongs either the doubled major third, or the major third with the superfluous fourth. Instead of this latter interval, the perfect fifth may also be taken.

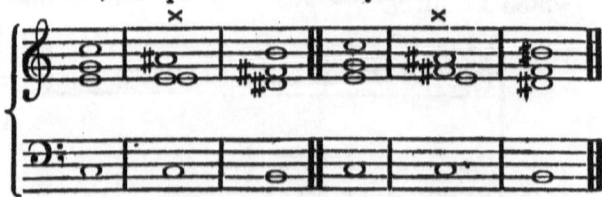

To the *diminished seventh* belong the minor third and the false fifth.

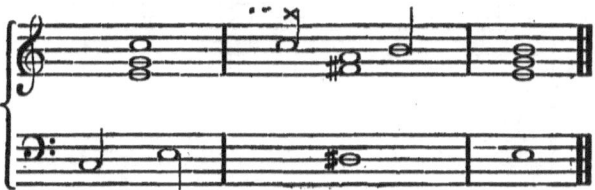

With the *minor seventh* we are already familiar.

To the *major seventh* belong the major second and the perfect fourth, to which, as a fifth part, the perfect fifth may also be added.

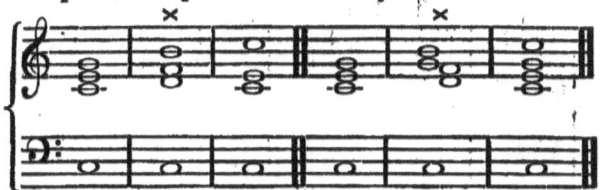

To the *diminished octave* are to be added the minor third and minor sixth.

You are already acquainted with the nature of the *perfect octave*, from the perfect common chord.

The *superfluous octave* is a mere passing note, and it may be accompanied by the major third and perfect fifth.

The *minor* and *major ninth* require the major third and perfect fifth by way of accompaniment, to which may also be added the minor seventh.

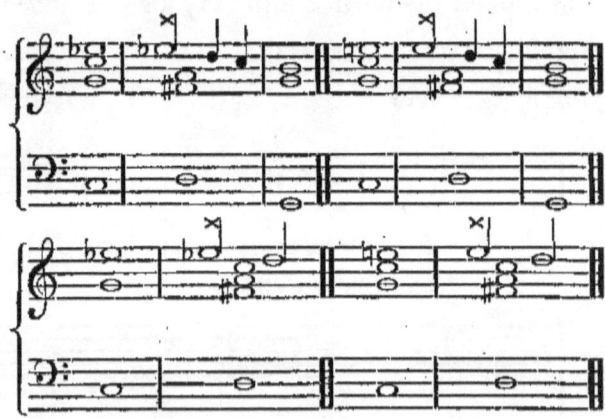

And from this you may perceive the difference between the *ninth* and the *second*.

Most of these chords have likewise their different positions; and in what manner these are formed, I have already explained in the preceding letters, in treating of the common chord and the chord of the seventh. But I must again repeat that these chords must be practised in all the keys, if you wish to derive any practical utility therefrom.

But enough on this subject. My view was only to give you a general idea of Harmony or Thorough-bass; and when you begin the study of it in a regular manner,—and I hear with pleasure that you are shortly about to do so, and that your worthy teacher has selected for this purpose the excellent Treatise on Harmony by *Reicha**,—all that I have hitherto said on the subject will serve to facilitate the acquirement of this science.

* As the works of Reicha have not yet appeared in an English dress, the Translator begs to recommend to the student who is desirous of acquiring a complete knowledge of harmony and composition, his miniature series of Musical Catechims, the contents of which are as follows:
No. 1. Catechism on Harmony and Thorough-bass.
No. 2. ——— on Counterpoint & Melody, or Rhythm.
No. 3. ——— on Double Counterpoint and Fugue.
No. 4. ——— on Writing for an Orchestra.
No. 5. ——— on the Invention, Exposition, and Development of Musical Ideas.
These little works are published, at two shillings each, by Messrs. R. Cocks and Co.
To these may be added, my Musical Grammar, adapted to the present state of the art, price 4s.—Albrechtsberger's celebrated Treatise on Harmony and Composition, translated by A. Merrick, 2 vols. 8vo. price 42s.—Cherubini's Course of Counterpoint and Fugue, 2 vols. 8vo. translated by Hamilton, price 42s.—and Fétis' Method of Accompaniment, translated by J. Bishop, price 12s.

LETTER X.

ON EXTEMPORANEOUS PERFORMANCE.

Dear Miss Cecilia,

You are aware that music is in some measure a species of language, by which may be expressed those passions and feelings with which the mind is burthened or affected.

It is also known to you that we are able to play on any musical instrument, *and more particularly on the pianoforte*, much which has neither been written down before, nor previously prepared or studied, but which is merely the fruit of a momentary and accidental inspiration. This is called *extemporizing*.

Such extemporaneous performances cannot naturally, and indeed ought not to assume the strict forms of written compositions; nay, the very freedom and inartificial nature of such productions gives them a peculiar charm; and many celebrated masters, such as *Beethoven* and *Hummel*, have particularly distinguished themselves in this art.

Although, for this purpose, and indeed for music in general, a certain share of natural talent is required, still extemporizing may be studied and practised according to certain principles; and I am convinced that any body, who has attained to more than a moderate skill in *playing*, is also capable, at least to a certain degree, of acquiring the art of playing extemporaneously. But for this purpose it is requisite to commence this sort of practice at an early period (which, alas! most players neglect); and that we should learn to indefatigably apply the experience which we have gained by studying the compositions of others, to our own extemporaneous performances.

At present, as your execution is so considerably formed, and as you are beginning to make a progress in thorough-bass, you should attempt, sometimes when alone, sometimes in the presence of your teacher, to connect together easy chords, short melodies, passages, scales, arpeggioed chords; or, which is much better, leave it to your fingers to effect this connection, according to their will and pleasure. For extemporizing possesses this singular and puzzling property, that reflection and attention are of scarcely any service in the matter. We must leave nearly every thing to the fingers and to chance.

At first, this will appear difficult to you; what you play will seem unconnected, or even incorrect; you will lose that courage and confidence in yourself which are so necessary to this purpose. But if you do not allow yourself to be frightened by this, and will repeat these attempts day after day, you will perceive that your powers will become more developed from week to week; and, with a more extended knowledge of thorough-bass, you will soon learn also to avoid faults against harmony.

At first, you must attempt to extemporize only short movements, somewhat similar to preludes or cadences. By degrees you must endeavour to extend these, by interweaving longer melodies, brilliant passages, arpeggioed chords, &c. If, in default of ideas of your own readily offering themselves, you should avail yourself of such as you have learned from other compositions, such assistance is always very excusable.

The scale-passages, and the chords of transition which connect them, are a good means of filling up any little chasm, when no melodious ideas happen to strike the player.

You know that all music may be reduced to simple chords. Just so, simple chords conversely serve as the ground-work on which to invent and play all sorts of melodies, passages, skips, embellishments, &c.

When you have devoted a considerable time to a rational practice in the way here pointed out, you will feel astonished at the great improvement, and the variety of applications of which the talent for extemporizing is capable.

You will find that nearly all the forms usual in composition are applicable to extempore-playing. Thus:

We may extemporize variations on themes chosen by ourselves or given for the purpose.

We may put together very interesting potpourris or fantasias from favorite motivos, combining them with brilliant passages, so as to form a striking ensemble.

We may also distinguish ourselves by extemporizing in strict four-part composition, or in the fugue style, &c. &c.

But for all this is required:

Great and highly cultivated facility and rapidity of finger, as well as a perfect command of all the keys, and of every mechanical difficulty. For you may easily imagine, Miss, that the happiest talent avails nothing, when the fingers are incapable of following and obeying its dictates. Besides this, it also requires an intimate acquaintance with the compositions of all the great composers; for only by this means can one's own talent be awakened, cultivated, and strengthened, so as to enable us to produce music of our own invention.

To this, as you know, must be added a thorough practical knowledge of harmony;

and, lastly,—as I repeat once more,—our own indefatigable and rationally applied industry.

Therefore, dear Miss, exercise yourself cheerfully and courageously in this very honorable branch of the art. If the labour is great, the pleasure and reward which you may gain thereby are still greater.

And now, Miss Cecilia, I announce to you, to your terror, that I shall very shortly be in your neighbourhood, that I shall visit you, and, with an awful, judge-like mien, convince myself in person of your diligence. That you will be greatly alarmed at this, I take to be a matter of course.

I now close the correspondence with which I have so long tormented you, and look with satisfaction towards the moment in which I shall be enabled in person to admire the unquestionably perfect cultivation of your very distinguished talent.

Accept also, for the last time, the *written* assurance of my unfeigned devotion.

Yours, &c.

FINIS.

www.ingramcontent.com/pod-product-compliance
Lightning Source LLC
Chambersburg PA
CBHW031226170426
43191CB00030B/289